WHERE DO ELECTRICITY COME FROM?

Where It Comes From

electricity [ih•lek•TRIS•uh•tee]
the supply of electric current to a house

coal [KOHL]
a black, solid mineral

coal mine[KOHL MINE]
the place where people
extract coal

electrician [ih•lek•TRISH•un]
a person who connects electricity to buildings

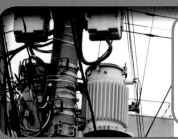

pole [POHL]
a tall, thin piece of wood or metal

resource [REE•zors]
a supply of something that can be used

substation [SUB•stay•shun]
a place where electricity is transformed

wire [WIRE]
a long, thin thread of metal

The electricity that comes
to your house
starts with a resource.

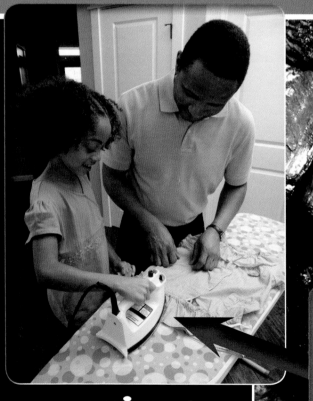

using

connecting

generating

resource

transforming

transmitting

Some resources used
to make electricity will run out.
Some resources won't run out.

Key

 = will run out
– non-renewable

= won't run out
– renewable

sun

wind

coal

house

oil

steam

water

The resources to make electricity are in different places.

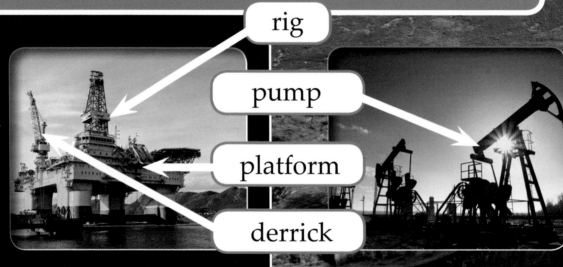

rig

pump

platform

derrick

off-shore oil field

on-shore oil field

You can find oil under the ground and under the seabed.

resources

solar panels

wind farm

nuclear power plant

hydro lake

geothermal area

coal mine

A resource like coal,
goes from a coal mine
to a power station.
The power station
uses the coal
to make electricity.

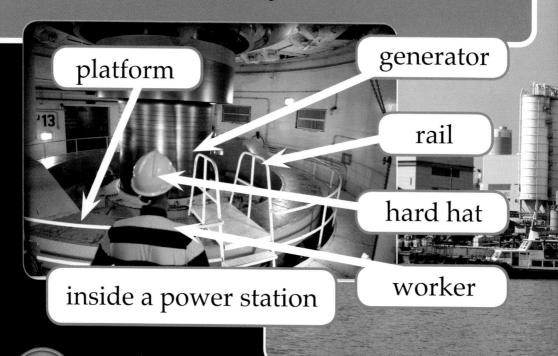

platform

generator

rail

hard hat

worker

inside a power station

generating

coal

This is a coal-fired power station.
It uses coal to generate electricity.

Electricity flows along wires
to a substation.
The electricity in these wires
is very strong.
The substation makes
the strong electricity weaker.

insulators

cables

transforming

wires

pylon

Electricity is transformed
at a substation.

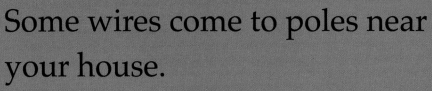

Some wires come to poles near your house.
Some wires come to your house underground.

After the electricity is transformed, it's transmitted along more wires.

transmitting

For some people, electricity comes from a pole to their house.

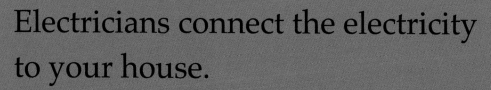

Electricians connect the electricity to your house.
They put in fuses.
They put in power outlets.
They put in switches.

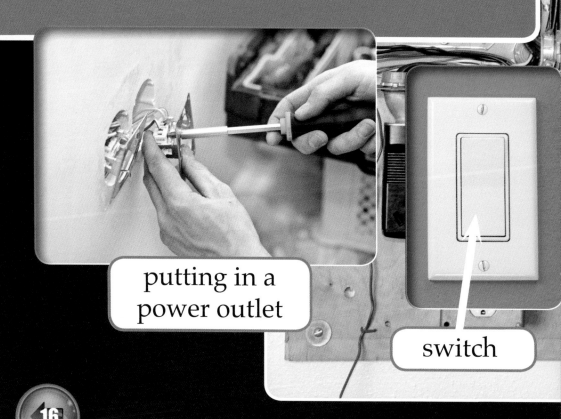

putting in a
power outlet

switch

connecting

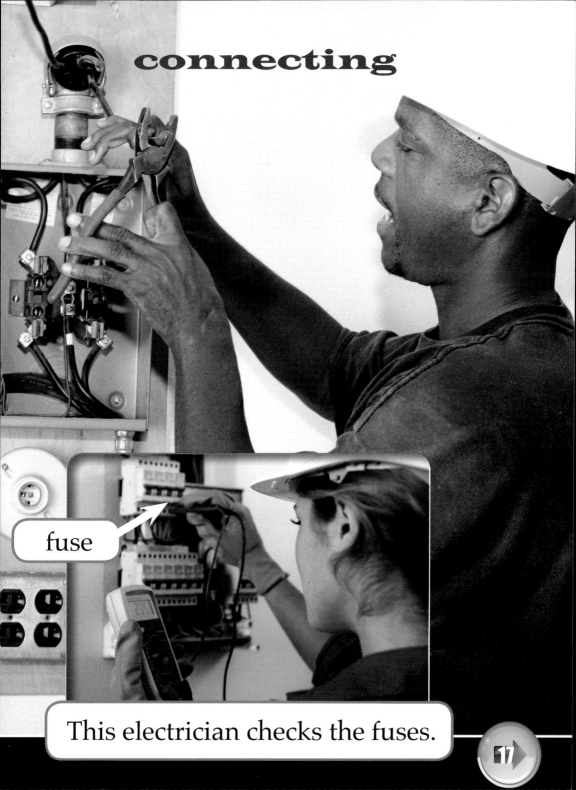

fuse

This electrician checks the fuses.

Now it's time to use the electricity.

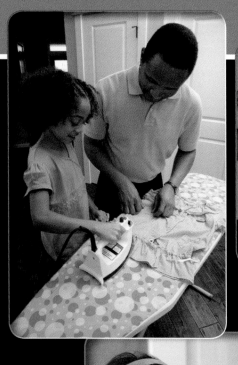

using electricity

People use electricity
in different ways.

Icons

An icon is like a sign. The picture represents a word, a concept, or an idea.

These icons show you ways of producing electricity.

solar power

nuclear power

oil rig

power station

transmitter

hydro dam

oil well

wind farm

coal mine

Extra Vocabulary

derrick
platform
pump
rig

resources

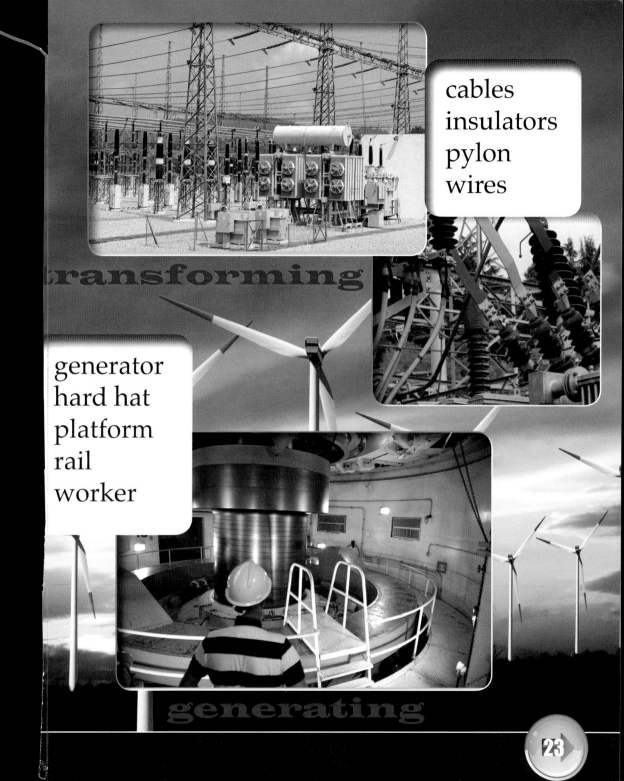

cables
insulators
pylon
wires

transforming

generator
hard hat
platform
rail
worker

generating

Critical Thinking

- What things in your house use electricity?
- What else is used to power appliances?
- How many ways can you think of to save electricity?

Concepts: Electricity

- Different resources can be used to generate electricity.
- Electricity is transmitted through wires.
- Strong electricity is transformed into weaker electricity as it nears cities.
- Electricians connect electricity to buildings.